W9-ANW-369

Diggers

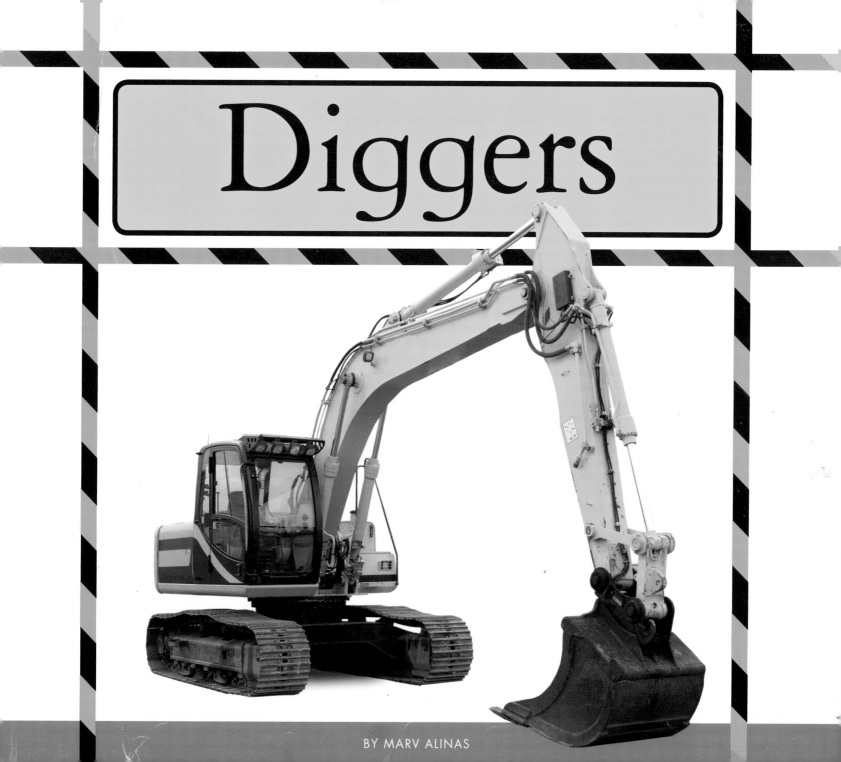

BY MARV ALINAS

The Child's World

Published by The Child's World®
1980 Lookout Drive • Mankato, MN 56003-1705
800-599-READ • www.childsworld.com

Acknowledgments
The Child's World®: Mary Berendes, Publishing Director
The Design Lab: Design
Jody Jensen Shaffer; Editing
Pamela J. Mitsakos: Photo Research

Photos
Bjørn Heller/iStock.com: cover, 1; bogdanhoda/
Shutterstock.com: 11; claffra/Shutterstock.com:
19; hans engbers/Shutterstock.com: 15; jennyt/
Shutterstock.com: 7; Jordan Rusev/iStock.com:
4; Marian Trotter/iStock.com: 20; michaeljung/
Shutterstock.com: 12; Robert Pernell/iStock.com: 16;
TFoxFoto/Shutterstock.com: 8

Copyright © 2014 by The Child's World®
All rights reserved. No part of this book may be
reproduced or utilized in any form or by any means
without written permission from the publisher.

ISBN 9781623239664
LCCN 2013947252

Printed in the United States of America
Mankato, MN
November, 2013
PA02190

Contents

Diggers are made of heavy metal and other materials.

Diggers can handle
many types of jobs.

This digger is tearing down an old house.

Diggers help clean up areas, too. Sometimes people tear down old buildings. Sometimes storms destroy buildings. Diggers help tear the buildings down. They help clean up the mess. They load the heavy trash on trucks. The trash goes to the dump.

What are the parts of a digger?

Diggers have a long arm called a **boom**. The end of the arm holds a big metal **bucket**. Together, the bucket and boom are called a **backhoe**. The digger pulls the boom in. That makes the bucket scoop up dirt.

boom

bucket

11

The driver must be careful with such a powerful machine!

The digger's body has a **cab** where the driver sits. The cab can spin all the way around. The cab has lots of **controls**. Some controls make the digger go forward and backward. Other controls move the boom and bucket.

Some diggers move around on wheels. But most diggers move on metal or rubber belts. These belts are called **crawler tracks**. Crawler tracks help diggers move over bumpy ground. They keep diggers from sinking in sand or mud.

A digger's crawler tracks are wide to keep the machine from tipping over.

Mini excavators can move around much easier.

Are there different kinds of diggers?

Diggers come in many shapes and sizes. Mini excavators are small diggers for small jobs. Bigger excavators are used for bigger jobs. You often see these diggers where people are building things.

Some excavators are very large. Dragline excavators often work in mines. They take huge bites of rock and dirt. The biggest diggers of all are bucket-wheel excavators. They are some of the biggest machines in the world!

These huge bucket-wheel excavators work in a coal mine.

Diggers can scoop a lot of dirt at one time!

Are diggers important?

Diggers are very important. They are used all over the world. They do all kinds of hard jobs. Nothing digs and scoops as well as a digger!

GLOSSARY

backhoe (BAK-ho) A backhoe is a digging scoop on a long arm.

boom (BOOM) A boom is a long arm that holds something up.

bucket (BUK-et) A digger's bucket is a big metal scoop.

cab (KAB) A machine's cab is the area where the driver sits.

controls (kun-TROHLZ) Controls are parts that people use to run a machine.

crawler tracks (KRAWL-ur TRAKS) Crawler tracks are metal belts that some machines use for moving.

excavators (EKS-kuh-vay-turs) Excavators are digging machines with a body that spins around.

mines (MYNZ) Mines are places where people dig rock from underground.

trenches (TRENCH-ez) Trenches are long, narrow ditches.

BOOKS

Deschamps, Nicola. *Digger*. New York: DK Publishing, 2006.

Gardner, Charlie (editor). *Diggers*. London/New York: DK Publishing, 2009.

Royston, Angela. *The Story of a Digger.* London: Kingfisher, 1998.

Young, Caroline. *Diggers and Cranes*. London: Usborne Publishing, 2005.

WEB SITES

Visit our Web site for lots of links about diggers: **childsworld.com/links**

Note to parents, teachers, and librarians: We routinely check our Web links to make sure they're safe, active sites—so encourage your readers to check them out!

INDEX

ABOUT THE AUTHOR

Marv Alinas has lived in Minnesota for over thirty years. When she's not reading or writing, Marv enjoys spending time with her dog and traveling to small river towns in northeastern Iowa and western Wisconsin.